This Book

presented to the

CHURCH
LIBRARY
IN MEMORY OF

Mark Weatherly

BY

Mr. & Mrs. Howard Nix

Code 4386-23, No. 3, Broadman Supplies, Nashville, Tenn. Printed in USA

Foreword for Mountain Songs

Whether we walk through valleys or along the ridges, all of us note the varied changes of each season. As we read the Psalms in this book, we will discover afresh the loving way God meets us at every turn through these seasons.

Each psalm and each photograph has been chosen carefully to portray various stages of our pilgrimage—the periods of despair, apathy, or pain as well as those of joy.

Like King David, we can turn to the Lord when we hurt because God meets our innermost needs before we even know they exist. God prepares us to receive the grace for what lies ahead. No matter what path He chooses for us—we are surrounded with God's promises for ultimate victory, and in any situation, songs of praise.

Mountain Songs is a delightful tapestry of nature photographs, daily Bible readings, and personal prayer meditations that bring comfort and inspiration. Many of the Scripture selections in this book are favorites of mine, and I am certain they will become favorites of yours, too. As you read this book, it is my prayer that whatever your need, you will discover some fresh thought to bring you unexpected encouragement.

by Ruth Bell Graham

PHOTOS BY:	PAGE:
Benny Alex:	42, 43, 46-47
Louis Bertrand:	3
Willi Burkhardt:	Cover, 6-7, 18-19, 20-21, 60-61, 62-63, 74—75
Siegfried Eigstler:	50-51, 52-53, 68-69
Bent Hansen:	16
Bildarchiv Huber:	4-5
Jørgen Vium Olesen:	12-13, 14, 17, 22-23, 26-27, 28-29, 32, 34-35, 38-39, 40-41, 48-49, 54-55, 56, 58-59, 66, 67, 70-71, 72-73
Otto Pfenninger:	76-77
Ulrik & Marco Schneiders:	78
Flemming Walsøe:	8-9, 10-11, 15, 24-25, 30, 31, 33, 44-45, 57, 64-65
Fred Wirz:	36-37

Mountain Songs
Daybreak Books are published by the Zondervan Publishing House
1415 Lake Drive, S.E., Grand Rapids, Michigan 49506
Copyright © 1981, 1982, 1988 by Forlaget Scandanavia
Noerregade 32, 1165, Copennagen K, Denmark

ISBN 0-310-54640-0

Edited by Jorgen Vium Olesen and Nia Jones
Text by Edith Schaeffer from L'Abri, and Common Sense,
Printed in Hong Kong by South Sea International Press Ltd.

MOUNTAIN SONGS

Selections from the Psalms with prayer meditations

Edited by Jørgen Vium Olesen and Nia Jones
Text by Edith Schaeffer
Scripture text from The Holy Bible, New International Version

Daybreak Books

Zondervan Publishing House
Grand Rapids, Michigan

For who is God,
except the Lord? And
who is a rock, except
our God? It is God who arms
me with strength, And makes my way
perfect. He makes my feet
like the feet of deer,
And sets me on my
high places.

What is man that
You are mindful of
him, And the son of man that
You visit him? For You have made him
a little lower than the angels,
And You have crowned him
with glory and honor.

5

Happy Are Those

Whatever he does propers.

**Blessed is the man who does not walk in the counsel of
the wicked or stand in the way of sinners or sit in the
seat of mockers.**

**But his delight is in the law of the Lord, and on his law
he meditates day and night.**

**He is like a tree planted by streams of water, which
yields its fruit in season and whose leaf does not wither.
Whatever he does prospers.**

**Not so the wicked! They are like chaff that the wind
blows away.**

**Therefore the wicked will not stand in the judgment,
nor sinners in the assembly of the righteous.**

**For the Lord watches over the way of the righteous, but
the way of the wicked will perish.**

*One night avalanches began to make
their way down the mountainside with
frightening rushes. We could hear the
roar at our chalet. . . . Sudden destruction
seemed very possible with the shifting,
unpredictable earth . . . and we realized
in a very vivid way that only an all-
powerful God could be depended upon to
take care of "all our needs."*

The Lord Reigns

I have installed my King on Zion, my holy hill.

**Why do the nations rage and the peoples plot in vain?
The kings of the earth take their stand and the rulers
gather together against the Lord and against his
Anointed One.
"Let us break their chains," they say, "and throw off
their fetters."
The One enthroned in heaven laughs; the Lord scoffs at
them.
Then he rebukes them in his anger and terrifies them in
his wrath, saying,
"I have installed my King on Zion, my holy hill."**

*One thing was becoming certain in our
minds. God had brought us to this little
village, at 3,100 feet altitude, to have a
chalet which would be L'Abri, or The
Shelter, a place to come and stay, for a
weekend or for a few days, with time to
ask questions and consider the answers
during walks in the mountains.*

Ask, and I Will Give You

Blessed are all who take refuge in him.

I will proclaim the decree of the Lord:
  He said to me, "You are my Son; today I have become your Father.
Ask of me, and I will make the nations your inheritance, the ends of the earth your possession.
You will rule them with an iron scepter; you will dash them to pieces like pottery."

Therefore, you kings, be wise; be warned, you rulers of the earth.
Serve the Lord with fear and rejoice with trembling.
Kiss the Son, lest he be angry and you be destroyed in your way, for his wrath can flare up in a moment.

"I'm not sure what Christianity meant to me before, but I know now what it means to me," she said earnestly as she accepted Christ as her Saviour and prayed. Her face was radiant, as she boarded the bus, but no more radiant than the feeling we had as we thrilled over this "new birth" in Chalet Mélèzes.

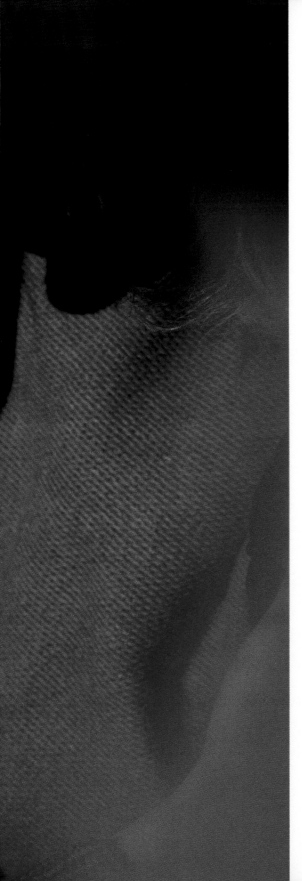

I Am Not Afraid

To the Lord I cry aloud, and he answers me from his holy hill.

O Lord, how many are my foes! How many rise up against me!
Many are saying of me, "God will not deliver him." — Selah
But you are a shield around me, O Lord, my Glorious One, who lifts up my head.
To the Lord I cry aloud, and he answers me from his holy hill. — Selah

I lie down and sleep; I wake again, because the Lord sustains me.
I will not fear the tens og thousands drawn up against me on every side.

Arise, O Lord! Deliver me, O my God! For you have struck all my enemies on the jaw; you have broken the teeth of the wicked.

From the Lord comes deliverance. May your blessing be on your people. — Selah.

We are individuals before God, and we believe He can deal with us as individuals. We have no binding human contract for life. Our binding contract is with God.

He Hears Me

The Lord will hear when I call to him.

Answer me when I call to you, O my righteous God.
Give me relief from my distress; be merciful to me and
hear my prayer.

How long, O men, will you turn my glory into shame?
How long will you love delusions and seek false gods?
Know that the Lord has set apart the godly for himself;
the Lord will hear when I call to him.

In your anger do not sin; when you are on your beds,
search your hearts and be silent. — Selah

Offer right sacrifices and trust in the Lord.

Many are asking, "Who can show us any good?" Let the
light of your face shine upon us, O Lord.
You have filled my heart with greater joy than when
their grain and new wine abound.
I will lie down and sleep in peace, for you alone, O
Lord, make me dwell in safety.

*God exists, and He is the One who has,
time after time, answered prayer in the
midst of well-nigh impossible
circumstances to bring about something
out of nothing.*

Voice in the Morning

You are not a God who takes pleasure in evil.

Give ear to my words, O Lord, consider my sighing.
Listgen to my cry for help, my King and my God, for to
you I pray.
Morning by morning, O Lord, you hear my voice;
morning by morning I lay my requests before you and
wait in expectation.

You are not a God who takes pleasure in evil; with you
the wicked cannot dwell.
The arrogant cannot stand in your presence; you hate all
who do wrong.
You destroy those who tell lies; bloodthirsty and
deceitful men the Lord abhors.

But I, by your great mercy, will come into your house;
in reverence will I bow down toward your holy temple.

*It was tremendous to breathe, the sun
felt different coming through it . . . and
what a clarity it gave to the view!*

Sing for Joy

But let all who take refuge in you be glad.

Lead me, O Lord, in your righteousness because of my enemies — make straight your way before me.

Not a word from their mouth can be trusted; their heart is filled with destruction. Their throat is an open grave; with their tongue they speak deceit.

Declare them guilty, O God! Let their intrigues be their downfall. Banish them for their many sins, for they have rebelled against you.

But let all who take refuge in you be glad; let them ever sing for joy. Spread your protection over them, that those who love your name may rejoice in you.

For surely, O Lord, you bless the righteous; you surround them with your favor as with a shield.

In the very midst of the most difficult times filled with anxiety, God has given us His pattern for the continuity of our relationship with Him. He does not leave us without explanation of what to do.

He shall be
like a tree
Planted by the
rivers of water,
That brings
forth its fruit
in its season,
Whose leaf
also shall
not wither;
And whatever
he does
shall prosper.

20

Rescue Me from Death

The Lord has heard my cry for mercy; the Lord accepts my prayer.

O Lord, do not rebuke me in your anger or discipline me in your wrath.

Be merciful to me, Lord, for I am faint; O Lord, heal me, for my bones are in agony.

My soul is in anguish. How long, O Lord, how long?

Turn, O Lord, and deliver me; save me because of your unfailing love.

No one remembers you when he is dead. Who praises you from the grave?

I am worn out from groaning; all night long I flood my bed with weeping and drench my couch with tears.

My eyes grow weak with sorrow; they fail because of all my foes.

Away from me, all you who do evil, for the Lord has heard my weeping.

The Lord has heard my cry for mercy; the Lord accepts my prayer.

May all my enemies be ashamed and dismayed; may they turn back in sudden disgrace.

If "eternal" depended on what a person had time left to do, or strength to do, or will-power to do, or emotions to feel, or talent to accomplish, or brilliance to understand, or money to pay for, or family line or merit, how sad a thing it would be to say, "Sorry, but this is not for you."

God, My Protector

O Lord my God, I take refuge in you; save and deliver me from all who pursue me.

O Lord my God, I take refuge in you; save and deliver me from all who pursue me,
or they will tear me like a lion and rip me to pieces with no one to rescue me.
O Lord my God, if I have done this and there is guilt on my hands —
if I have done evil to him who is at peace with me or without cause have robbed my foe —
then let my enemy pursue and overtake me; let him trample my life to the ground and make me sleep in the dust. — Selah
Arise, O Lord, in your anger; rise up against the rage of my enemies. Awake, my God; decree justice.
Let the assembled peoples gather around you. Rule over them from on high;
let the Lord judge the peoples. Judge me, O Lord, according to my righteousness, according to my integrity, O Most High.
O righteous God, who searches minds and hearts, bring to an end the violence of the wicked and make the righteous secure.

When people put themselves into the hands of the Master Technician—that is, God their Savior and Creator—they may expect constant help. We go "out of tune," or become "harsh" so quickly. We need to come to the Master to be "tuned" with His strength put into us, substituted for our weakness.

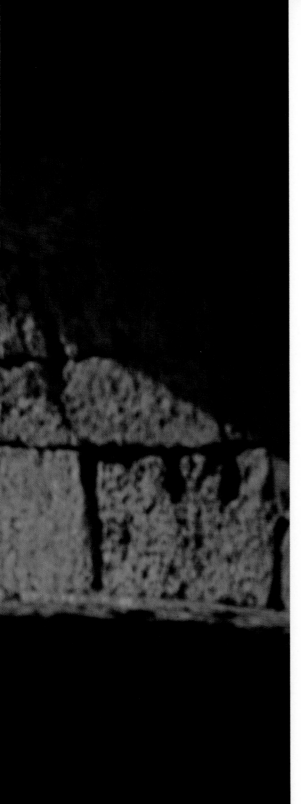

Consequences of Evil

I will give thanks to the Lord because of his righteousness.

My shield is God Most High, who saves the upright in heart.
God is a righteous judge, a God who expresses his wrath every day.
If he does not relent, he will sharpen his sword; he will bend and string his bow.
He has prepared his deadly weapons; he makes ready his flaming arrows.

He who is pregnant with evil and conceives trouble gives birth to disillusionment.
He who digs a hole and scoops it out falls into the pit he has made.
The trouble he causes recoils on himself; his violence comes down on his own head.

I will give thanks to the Lord because of his righteousness and will sing praise to the name of the Lord Most High.

Although God is perfect and does not make mistakes, human beings are even prone to go off limits in making judgments of God's perfect compassion, love, goodness and wisdom and criticizing God or declaring that God has done something He has not done at all.

Children's Song

How majestic is your name in all the earth!

O Lord, our.Lord, how majestic is your name in all the
earth!
You have set your glory above the heavens.
From the lips of children and infants you have ordained
praise because of your enemies, to silence the foe and
the avenger.

When I consider your heavens, the work of your fingers,
the moon and the stars, which you have set in place,
what is man that you are mindful of him, the son of man
that you care for him?
You made him a little lower than the heavenly beings
and crowned him with glory and honor.
You made him ruler over the works of your hands; you
put everything under his feet:
all flocks and herds, and the beasts of the field,
the birds of the air, and the fish of the sea, all that swim
the paths of the seas.

O Lord, our Lord, how majestic is your name in all the
earth!

*There is Someone at home in the
universe. There is Someone to look up
to. There is a light in the darkness.
There is a door in the wall. There is
truth to be found.*

Tell of Wonderful Things

The Lord is a refuge for the oppressed, for you,
Lord, have never forsaken those who seek you.

I will praise you, O Lord, with all my heart; I will tell of
all your wonders.
I will be glad and rejoice in you; I will sing praise to your
name, O Most High.
My enemies turn back; they stumble and perish before
you.
For you have upheld my right and my cause; you have
sat on your throne, judging righteously.
You have rebuked the nations and destroyed the
wicked; you have blotted out their name for ever and
ever.
Endless ruin has overtaken the enemy, you have
uprooted their cities; even the memory of them has
perished.
The Lord reigns forever; He has established his throne
for judgment.
He will judge the world in righteousness; he will govern
the peoples with justice.
The Lord is a refuge for the oppressed, a stronghold in
times of trouble.
Those who know your name will trust in you, for you,
Lord, have never forsaken those who seek you.

What about the future? Not one of us
would know any more than we did in the
beginning. But we know this. L'Abri is
God's plan, of that we are convinced. He
will continue it in the form in which He
has planned it, if we do not hinder Him
by letting self-will get in the way.

God Does Not Forget

He does not ignore the cry of the afflicted.

Sing praises to the Lord, enthroned in Zion; proclaim
among the nations what he has done.
For he who avenges blood remembers; he does not
ignore the cry of the afflicted.
O Lord, see how my enemies persecute me! Have mercy
and lift me up from the gates of death,
that I may declare your praises in the gates of the
Daughter of Zion and there rejoice in your salvation.
The nations have fallen into the pit they have dug; their
feet are caught in the net they have hidden.
The Lord is known by his justice; the wicked are
ensnared by the work of their hands. — Selah
The wicked return to the grave, all the nations that
forget God.
But the needy will not always be forgotten, nor the hope
of the afflicted ever perish.
Arise, O Lord, let not man triumph; let the nations be
judged in your presence.
Strike them with terror, O Lord; let the nations know
they are but men. — Selah

*If we believe what God has said, there is
hope, hope singing through with a music
that eases the pain. Hope that promises,
"This isn't the end; there is something
ahead. Things can be put back together
again someday." We need now really to
believe God, and act upon that belief.*

In Times of Trouble

Why, O Lord, do you stand far off? Why do you hide yourself in times of trouble?

Why, O Lord, do you stand far off? Why do you hide yourself in times of trouble?

In his arrogance the wicked man hunts down the weak, who are caught in the schemes he devises.

He boasts of the cravings of his heart; he blesses the greedy and reviles the Lord.

In his pride the wicked does not seek him; in all his thoughts there is no room for God.

His ways are always prosperous; he is haughty and your laws are far from him; he sneers at all his enemies.

He says to himself, "Nothing will shake me; I'll always be happy and never have trouble."

His mouth is full of curses and lies and threats; trouble and evil are under his tongue.

He lies in wait near the villages; from ambush he murders the innocent, watching in secret for his victims.

He lies in wait like a lion in cover; he lies in wait to catch the helpless; he catches the helpless and drags them off in his net.

His victims are crushed, they collapse; they fall under his strength.

He says to himself, "God has forgotten; he covers his face and never sees."

I read the paper with its message that had been phoned from the telegraph office in Lausanne and written down in Liselotte's handwriting. . . . The tears flowed suddenly, and my first cry was, "Oh, but I wanted to tell her about . . . I wanted to write her tomorrow and. . . ." There is, was, the wall of separation that death puts up against communication! It's this that the Bible is talking about when it says that Jesus came to have victory over death, the horrible enemy which was a result of sin.

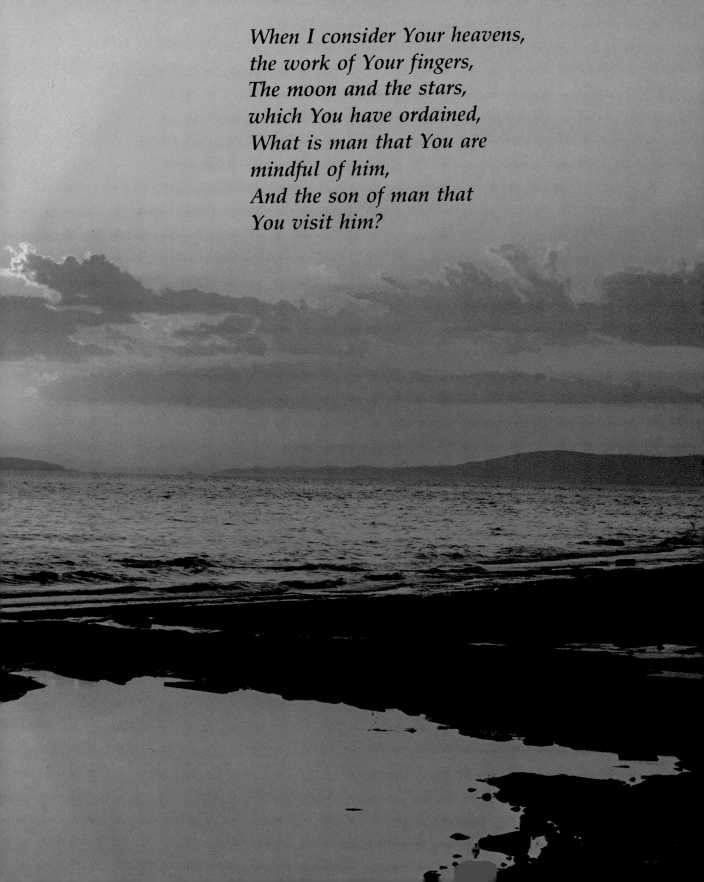

When I consider Your heavens,
the work of Your fingers,
The moon and the stars,
which You have ordained,
What is man that You are
mindful of him,
And the son of man that
You visit him?

Those with Needs

O Lord, you encourage them, and you listen to
their cry, defending the fatherless and the
oppressed.

Arise, Lord! Lift up your hand, O God. Do not forget
the helpless.
Why does the wicked man revile God? Why does he say
to himself, "He won't call me to account"?
But you, O God, do see trouble and grief; you consider
it to take it in hand. The victim commits himself to you;
you are the helper of the fatherless.
Break the arm of the wicked and evil man; call him to
account for his wickedness that would not be found out.

The Lord is King for ever and ever; the nations will
perish from his land.
You hear, O Lord, the desire of the afflicted; you
encourage them, and you listen to their cry, defending
the fatherless and the oppressed, in order that man, who
is of the earth, may terrify no more.

Those of us who are Workers at L'Abri
have established our purpose as this: "To
show forth by demonstration in our life
and work, the existence of God." We
have, in other words, decided to live on
the basis of prayer in several realms, so
that we might demonstrate to any who
care to look, the existence of God.

Safety

In the Lord I take refuge.

In the Lord I take refuge. How then can you say to me:
"Flee like a bird to your mountain.
For look, the wicked bend their bows; they set their
arrows against the strings to shoot from the shadows at
the upright in heart.
When the foundations are being destroyed, what can the
righteous do?"
The Lord is in his holy temple; the Lord is on his
heavenly throne. He observes the sons of men; his eyes
examine them.
The Lord examines the righteous, but the wicked and
those who love violence his soul hates.
On the wicked he will rain fiery coals and burning sulfur;
a scorching wind will be their lot.

For the Lord is righteous, he loves justice; upright men
will see his face.

*We are not to run away from God,
shaking our fist at Him and screaming.
We are to run to Him when we are
shaking with grief or trembling with fear.*

The Promises of God

"Because of the oppression of the weak and the groaning of the needy, I will now arise," says the Lord. "I will protect them from those who malign them."

Help, Lord, for the godly are no more; the faithful have vanished from among men.
Everyone lies to his neighbor; their flattering lips speak with deception.

May the Lord cut off all flattering lips and every boastful tongue that says,
"We will triumph with our tongues;
we own our lips — who is our master?"
Because of the oppression of the weak and the groaning of the needy, I will now arise," says the Lord. "I will protect them from those who malign them."
And the words of the Lord are flawless, like silver refined in a furnace of clay, purified seven times.

O Lord, you will keep us safe and protect us from such people forever.
The wicked freely strut about when what is vile is honored among men.

When you thrill with the love of God expressed in that wonderful tenor solo from Mendelssohn's Elijah, *"If with all thine heart ye truly seek me, ye shall surely find Me—thus saith the Lord—thus saith the Lord," remember that God is speaking to that whole nation in a time of their turning away deliberately.*

When God Hides Himself

But I trust in your unfailing love.

How long, O Lord? Will you forget me forever? How long will you hide your face from me?
How long must I wrestle with my thoughts and every day have sorrow in my heart? How long will my enemy triumph over me?
Look on me and answer, O Lord my God. Give light to my eyes, or I will sleep in death;
my enemy will say, "I have overcome him," and my foes will rejoice when I fall.

But I trust in your unfailing love; my heart rejoices in your salvation.
I will sing to the Lord, for he has been good to me.

Jesus is entrusting us to make truth known in spite of opposition and persecution. He is letting us know that whatever we go through in our lives, there will be nothing He cannot understand.

Expectations

Oh, that salvation for Israel would come out of Zion!

The fool says in his heart, "There is no God." They are corrupt, their deeds are vile; there is no one who does good.

The Lord looks down from heaven on the sons of men to see if there are any who understand, any who seek God.

All have turned aside, they have together become corrupt; there is no one who does good, not even one.

Will evildoers never learn — those who devour my people as men eat bread and who do not call on the Lord?

There they are, overwhelmed with dread, for God is present in the company of the righteous.

You evildoers frustrate the plans of the poor, but the Lord is their refuge.

Oh, that salvation for Israel would come out of Zion! When the Lord restores the fortunes of his people, let Jacob rejoice and Israel be glad!

The most precious thing a human being has to give is time. There is so very little of it, after all, in a life. Minutes in an hour, hours in a day, days in a week, weeks in a year, years in a life. It all goes so swiftly.

Safe from Enemies

He who does these things will never be shaken.

Lord, who may dwell in your sanctuary? Who may live on your holy hill?

He whose walk is blameless and who does what is righteous, who speaks the truth from his heart and has no slander on his tongue, who does his neighbor no wrong and casts no slur on his fellow man, who despises a vile man but honors those who fear the Lord, who keeps his oath even when it hurts, who lends his money without usury and does not accept a bribe against the innocent.

He who does these things will never be shaken.

We are to ask for stength and grace for our own difficult moments a moment at a time, but our understanding and sympathy is to be growing constantly.

All I Need

"You are my Lord; apart from you I have no good thing."

Keep me safe, O God, for in you I take refuge.

I said to the Lord, "You are my Lord; apart from you I have no good thing."

As for the saints who are in the land, they are the glorious ones in whom is all my delight.

The sorrows of those will increase who run after other gods. I will not pour out their libations of blood or take up their names on my lips.

Lord, you have assigned me my portion and my cup; you have made my lot secure.

The boundary lines have fallen for me in pleasant places; surely I have a delightful inheritance.

I will praise the Lord, who counsels me; even at night my heart instructs me.

"God's guidance." "God led us." What meaningless phrases these must be to anyone who thinks there is no God; or that if there is, He is not personal and so could not be contacted by any sort of real communication; and that if He could, He would surely not care about any such insignificant speck in the universe as one human being.

O Lᴏʀᴅ, our Lord,
How excellent is Your name
in all the earth!

Joy in His Presence

I have set the Lord always before me.

I have set the Lord always before me. Because he is at my right hand, I will not be shaken.

Therefore my heart is glad and my tongue rejoices; my body also will rest secure,

because you will not abandon me to the grave, nor will you let your Holy One see decay.

You have made known to me the path of life; you will fill me with joy in your presence, with eternal pleasures at your right hand.

God is perfect. Our Heavenly Father, our Friend and Shepherd; our Intercessor Jesus Christ; our Comforter the Holy Spirit are each perfect!

The Lord Lives!

O Lord, give ear to my prayer — it does not rise from deceitful lips.

Hear, O Lord, my righteous plea; listen to my cry. Give ear to my prayer — it does not rise from deceitful lips. May my vindication come from you; may your eyes see what is right.

Though you probe my heart and examine me at night, though you test me, you will find nothing; I have resolved that my mouth will not sin. As for the deeds of men — by the word of your lips I have kept myself from the ways of the violent. My steps have held to your paths; my feet have not slipped.

I do want to praise You, O God, with a praise that will bring joy to You, and I want my love to grow during my short lifetime. Please don't let me waste the time that I have to praise You with my lips. As I tell You I do really love You, may these words be acceptable to You because they are more real to me day by day. O Lord, I love You.

Wonderful Love

O God, give ear to me and hear my prayer.

I call on you, O God, for you will answer me; give ear
to me and hear my prayer.
Show the wonder of your great love, you who save by
your right hand those who take refuge in you from their
foes.

Keep me as the apple of your eye; hide me in the
shadow of your wings
from the wicked who assail me, from my mortal enemies
who surround me.

They close up their callous hearts, and their mouths
speak with arrogance.
They have tracked me down, they now surround me,
with eyes alert, to throw me to the ground.
They are like a lion hungry for prey, like a great lion
crouching in cover.
Rise up, O Lord, confront them, bring them down;
rescue me from the wicked by your sword.
O Lord, by your hand save me from such men, from
men of this world whose reward is in this life.

You still the hunger of those you cherish; their sons
have plenty, and they store up wealth for their children.
And I — in righteousness I will see your face; when I
awake, I will be satisfied with seeing your likeness.

*Every day we should search for someone
to really serve in love, remembering that
only in that way can practical kindnesses
be given directly to the Lord.*

Rescue in Trouble

I love you, O Lord, my strength.

The Lord is my rock, my fortress and my deliverer; my God is my rock, in whom I take refuge. He is my shield and the horn of my salvation, my stronghold. I call to the Lord, who is worthy of praise, and I am saved from my enemies.

In the small measure in which we have come to put self aside, and to wait for God's direction, we have found, and will find, reality in a two-way communication with God.

Majesty of God

From his temple he heard my voice.

The cords of death entangled me; the torrents of destruction overwhelmed me.
The cords of the grave coiled around me; the snares of death confronted me.
In my distress I called to the Lord; I cried to my God for help. From his temple he heard my voice; my cry came before him, into his ears.

The earth trembled and quaked, and the foundations of the mountains shook; they trembled because he was angry.
Smoke rose from his nostrils; consuming fire came from his mouth, burning coals blazed out of it.
He parted the heavens and came down; dark clouds were under his feet.
He mounted the cherubim and flew; he soared on the wings of the wind.
He made darkness his covering, his canopy around him — the dark rain clouds of the sky.
Out of the brightness of his presence clouds advanced, with hailstones and bolts of lightning.

This is not a life of ease, but a life of tremendous excitement, in between the struggles; excitement because of finding that we are in contact with the supernatural today.

Entering God's Presence

He brought me out into a spacious place. He
rescued me.

The Lord thundered from heaven; the voice of the Most
High resounded.
He shot his arrows and scattered the enemies, great
bolts of lightning and routed them.
The valleys of the sea were exposed and the foundations
of the earth laid bare at your rebuke, O Lord, at the
blast of breath from your nostrils.
He reached down from on high and took hold of me; he
drew me out of deep waters.
He rescued me from my powerful enemy, from my foes,
who were too strong for me.
They confronted me in the day of my disaster, but the
Lord was my support.
He brought me out into a spacious place; he rescued me
because he delighted in me.

As summer drew near, our French
teacher urged us to go to the mountains.
"All Swiss do. It is important for the
children's health to have a change in
altitude," she said.

I took a trip to the village she suggested,
Champéry, and visited one or two chalets
which were for rent, selecting a lovely
one full of balconies and geranium
window-boxes. . . . We looked out of
windows now to see the mountains
directly across from us, looking at
waterfalls and cliffs rather than peaks or
sky. It was necessary to go out to the
balcony to see the sky.

Light in Darkness

With my God I can scale a wall.

The Lord has dealt with me according to my
righteousness; according to the cleanness of my hands
he has rewarded me.
For I have kept the ways of the Lord; I have not done
evil by turning from my God.
All his laws are before me; I have not turned away from
his decrees.
I have been blameless before him and have kept myself
from sin.
The Lord has rewarded me according to my
righteousness, according to the cleanness of my hands in
his sight.
To the faithful you show yourself faithful, to the pure
you show yourself pure, but to the crooked you show
yourself shrewd.
You save the humble but bring low those whose eyes are
haughty.
You, O Lord, keep my lamp burning; my God turns my
darkness into light.
With your help I can advance against a troop; with my
God I can scale a wall.
As for God, his way is perfect; the word of the Lord is
flawless. He is a shield for all who take refuge in him.

*One can't put an hour of talking to God
in a paragraph, but it is important for
you to know that it was an hour, and
not a sentence; and that there is a two-
way communication in prayer, and the
reality of the Holy Spirit's work in a
Christian during the actual time of
praying. . . . It was then that suddenly I
became flooded with a surge of assurance
that God can do anything, nothing is
impossible to Him.*

I have set the L<small>ORD</small> *always before me;*
Because He is at my right hand
I shall not be moved.

Foothold on the Mountains

Who is the Rock except our God?

For who is God besides the Lord? And who is the Rock except our God?
It is God who arms me with strength and makes my way perfect.
He makes my feet like the feet of a deer; he enables me to stand on the heights.
He trains my hands for battle; my arms can bend a bow of bronze.
You give me your shield of victory, and your right hand sustains me; you stoop down to make me great.
You broaden the path beneath me, so that my ankles do not turn.

I pursued my enemies and overtook them; I did not turn back till they were destroyed.
I crushed them so that they could not rise; they fell beneath my feet.
You armed me with strength for battle; you made my adversaries bow at my feet.
You made my enemies turn their back in flight, and I destroyed my foes.
They cried for help, but there was no one to save them — to the Lord, but he did not answer.
I beat them as fine as dust borne on the wind; I poured them out like mud in the streets.

"I can't walk, Mommy . . . I can't walk!"
he waited, with a question in his voice.

"Indomitable will forced him to keep trying, for after that first wail over not walking, he never mentioned it again, but just determined *to pick himself up and go on no matter how many times he fell. . . . Franky in his bitterest moments has recognized as good results which have come out of tragedy.*

God's Way

You exalted me above my foes.

You have delivered me from the attacks of the people; you have made me the head of nations; people I did not know are subject to me.
As soon as they hear me, they obey me; foreigners cringe before me.
They all lose heart; they come trembling from their strongholds.
The Lord lives! Praise be to my Rock! Exalted be God my Savior!
He is the God who avenges me, who subdues nations under me,
who saves me from my enemies. You exalted me above my foes; from violent men you rescued me.
Therefore I will praise you among the nations, O Lord; I will sing praises to your name.
He gives his king great victories; he shows unfailing kindness to his anointed, to David and his descendants forever.

There are, and always will be, many places for improvement in our struggle to be honest before God, hour by hour, day by day, month by month. So there are, and will be many places for improvement in that which is to be seen by other eyes.

God's Glory in Creation

Day after day they pour forth speech; night after
night they display knowledge.

The heavens declare the glory of God; the skies
proclaim the work of his hands.
Day after day they pour forth speech; night after night
they display knowledge.
There is no speech or language where their voice is not
heard.
Their voice goes out into all the earth, their words to the
ends of the world.
In the heavens he has pitched a tent for the sun,
which is like a bridegroom coming forth from his
pavilion, like a champion rejoicing to run his course.
It rises at one end of the heavens and makes its circuit to
the other; nothing is hidden from its heat.

In these words we learn that the whole
of creation communicates something.
More of creation can now be inspected
as man brings some of the moon rock
back with him; more can be seen through
a telescope or with the naked eye. All
that we see in the stars and the planets,
in the sun and the moon, are not only
there for useful reasons, but also as an
art form, a communication of the glory
and the greatness of the Artist.

I will praise You, O Lord,
with my whole heart;
I will tell of all
Your marvelous works.

The Lord is my
rock and my fortress and
my deliverer; My God, my strength,
in whom I will trust; My shield and the horn
of my salvation, my stronghold. I will call upon the Lord,
who is worthy to be praised; So shall I be saved
from my enemies. The pangs of death
encompassed me, And the floods of
ungodliness made me afraid.